GETTING INTO NATURE™

GETTING INTO NATURE™

Olive Trees

INSIDE AND OUT

Text by Andrew Hipp
Illustrations by Fiammetta Dogi

The Rosen Publishing Group's
PowerKids Press™
New York

*For Glen and Luanne Clifton, who shared their home
and their friendship and gave me a jar of delicious home-cured olives*

Published in 2004 in North America
by The Rosen Publishing Group, Inc.
29 East 21st Street, New York, NY 10010

First Edition

Book Design:
Andrea Dué s.r.l., Florence, Italy

Illustrations:
Fiammetta Dogi and Studio Stalio
Map by Alessandro Bartolozzi

Scientific advice for botanical illustrations:
Riccardo Maria Baldini

Library of Congress Cataloging-in-Publication Data
Hipp, Andrew.
Olive trees inside and out / Andrew Hipp.
    p. cm. — (Getting into nature)
Summary: Describes the history of olive trees and the structure,
cultivation, and use of olives.
Includes bibliographical references (p.) and index.
ISBN 0-8239-4207-4 (library binding)
1. Olive—Juvenile literature. [1. Olive.] I. Title. II. Series.
SB367.H69 2004
634'.63—dc22
                                                              2003015534

Manufactured in Italy by Eurolitho S.p.A., Milan

Contents

The Olive Tree

Olive trees grow slowly and live for a long time, though they generally do not grow taller than 40 feet (12 meters). There are olive trees alive today that were alive in the time of Jesus. Olive trees that are hundreds of years old are not uncommon. They can live through **droughts** and often grow in dry, rocky soils. Their wood is strong and resists both rot and sickness.

Olive trees are important to people and other animals. They supply people with lamp oil, with a moisturizer to keep their skin healthy, and with food. Birds and other animals eat olives and scatter the seeds.

If you live in a place that enjoys Mediterranean-style weather—dry, warm, and sunny during the summer, with rain falling mainly in the winter—you most likely have olives growing in your area.

Olive tree
(Olea europaea)

How Olives Traveled the World

The first people to taste olives lived in the Mediterranean area and the Middle East more than 10,000 years ago.

Olives at first grew only on a wild bush called oleaster. Olives became useful to many societies because they could be pressed to make a healthy and useful oil or prepared for eating. Six thousand years ago, people were **cultivating** olive trees near Greece and Turkey. Two thousand years ago, Greek travelers began bringing olives to Italy, France, Spain, and Tunisia. Between AD 1500 and 1800, Spanish **missionaries** planted olive trees in Cuba, Hispaniola, Mexico, and California. Today, there are about 800 million olive trees growing all over the world.

Above: This Roman artwork shows a person gathering olives that have fallen from the nearby trees.

PORTUGAL

FRANCE

SPAIN

ITALY

M e d i t e r r a n e a n

GREECE

TURKEY

NORTH AFRICA

S e a

ISRAEL

WHERE OLIVE TREES GREW IN ANCIENT TIMES

Opposite, far left:
An ancient amphora,
or vase, used to store
oil and wine.

Right: This Tuscan
olive tree is about
3,000 years old.

Below: A Roman
stone carving
shows an
olive press.

Life in Dry Places

Olive trees are able to live through droughts that would kill most other fruit trees. Roots of olive trees do not become withered, or dry and weakened, in dry seasons. This allows the roots to stay connected to bits of soil, which are coated with a thin layer of water. The trees let out stored water to keep cool, just like people and many other animals sweat to cool down on a hot day. Olive leaves are covered with scales that help keep the plant from drying out. Olive trees also continue to grow roots when dry weather slows down leaf growth. In this way, the trees search continuously for water under the ground.

Right: An olive tree's roots can send up new growth to take the place of a trunk that freezes or is cut down. An olive tree may have roots that are many hundreds of years old, while its trunk may be just a baby.

Above:
Most olives are
still grown in the
Mediterranean area and the
Middle East. The Mediterranean
countries of Spain, Italy, and
Greece produce 80 percent of
the world's olive oil. The olives
at top right are young and green,
while the ones at top left are
beginning to ripen and darken
with age.

Right: A Ligurian olive tree
in Italy.

Growing Olives

Olive growers cut strong, young branches off of olive trees and place the ends into wet soil. Within a month or two, the branches begin to form roots. When many roots have formed, the branches are **transplanted** in orchards, or fields of trees, where they grow into trees. When they are several years old, the olive trees will begin to produce olives. Some kinds of olive trees have trouble growing from transplanted branches. Instead, branches of these kinds of olive trees are **grafted** onto the trunk, or thick base, of an olive tree that grows easily from seeds. Many trees are grown from seeds just to provide trunks for grafting the olive trees that are hard to transplant.

Right: Olive trees must be pruned, or cut back, occasionally. This helps control the amount of olives grown and shape the tree in a way that makes collecting the fruit easier. At right are some pruning tools and a recently pruned orchard. All of this labor helps create the ripe olives pictured here.

This is a typical Moroccan olive tree.

ripe olives

pruning tools

This is what an olive orchard looks like after pruning.

Olives are Fruits

Olives are a special kind of fruit called a **drupe**. The soft part of a drupe is called the flesh. Olive flesh is green when it is young, and it becomes dark purple or black as it ages. Every drupe has a hard pit, which holds a seed. Inside the seed is an **embryo** that can grow up to look like the plant that created it. A single olive tree may grow as many as 500,000 olives. Olives are a tasty treat for birds and other animals, which eat the fruit and carry and scatter the seeds.

Leccino

The fruit pictured on these pages show several varieties of Italian olives.

Below, left and opposite, top right are drawings from an early eighteenth century study of Tuscan olives.

Pendolino

Frantoiano

Santa Caterina

Ascolana

Moraiolo

Uovo di
piccione

13

Olives Come from Perfect Flowers

Small white flowers with four petals grow on olive trees. Every olive tree has both male flowers and **perfect flowers**.

Male flowers make **pollen**, which is carried by wind or bees to the perfect flowers. Perfect flowers make pollen, too. Unlike the male flowers, however, they also have **stigmas**. Stigmas catch pollen and help guide the pollen tube toward the **ovary**. The pollen tube **fertilizes** an **ovule** that is inside the ovary. After it is fertilized, the ovule can become an olive seed. The ovary wall becomes the olive flesh and the hard outer wall of the pit.

The flowers on these pages are from trees and shrubs of the Oleaceae family, which also includes olive trees.

Border forsythia
(Forsythia x intermedia)

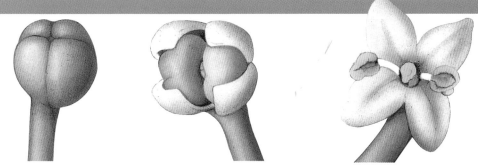

Above: These are the three stages of growth of an olive flower.

Above: These drawings show the gradual growth of the flowers of a Barnea olive tree.

Golden privet
(*Ligustrum vulgare*)

Common lilac
(*Syringa vulgaris*)

Most olive trees will produce more olives if their flowers are fertilized by pollen from a different kind of olive tree. For this reason, olive growers often plant several kinds of olive trees together in one orchard.

15

Harvesting Olives

People **harvest** olives at different times of the year, depending on the farmers' tastes and what the olives will be used for. Olives harvested early have green, bitter fruit, but many people like the taste of the fruit and the oil that early olives make. Olives harvested later in the year are darker, have a higher oil content, and are less bitter. But olives harvested later in the year may be harmed by frost or bugs.

Today, many olives are harvested using machines that beat the olives from the trees. Olives and the leaves that fall with them are caught beneath the trees in nets.

Opposite: Nets are spread beneath the trees to collect olives that have been shaken off the branches. Olives can also be gathered by "combing" the branches (*inset*).

Bottom: A drawing in a fourteenth-century book shows a man and a woman harvesting an olive tree.

Many people still harvest olives the old-fashioned way—by beating the branches with long sticks or picking the olives from the tree by hand. This is how olives were harvested for thousands of years, before electric-and gas-powered harvesting machines were invented.

Olives for Eating

The flesh of an olive just picked from the tree contains a **chemical** that makes it taste bitter. For this reason, olives must be cured, or prepared, before they are eaten. Olives are cured by soaking them in water for many weeks to draw the bitterness out of their flesh. Many people use salty water, sometimes with garlic or other spices. Others use fresh water. A chemical called **lye** is often used to get the bitterness out of green olives. Canned California "black olives" that we buy in the store are actually green olives blackened by a combination of lye and air that is bubbled through the water.

Bottom, left: Olives, olive oil, and bread form a common Mediterranean snack.

Below: Traditional clay jars like this one are still used today to store olives.

Because of the bitterness of olive flesh, olives were most likely first used for oil rather than eating. Olive oil itself was first used in lamps and to keep skin healthy, rather than for cooking. Later, however, olives and olive oil became among the most important elements of the Mediterranean diet, as they still are today.

Olive Oil

Olive oil is produced by pressing olives with a giant wheel made of stone or metal. The pressed olives are spread onto mats, and the oil is either allowed to drip from the olives on its own or squashed out under a giant weight. Sometimes hot water is added to the pressed olives to break up the olive cells, which hold drops of oil. The oil is then allowed to settle for several days. The good oil floats to the top and is spooned off. Water and olive bits stay at the bottom of the bucket. Today, machines often spin the oil and water combination at very high speeds, separating water and olive bits from oil very quickly. However, many people feel that the oil does not taste as good when it is prepared this way.

Opposite: This is an old-fashioned oil mill, like the one labeled below.

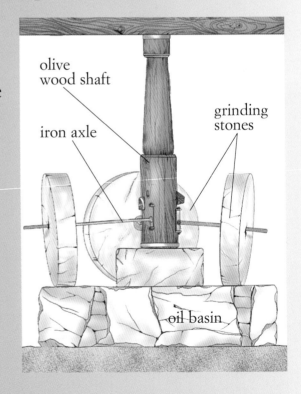

olive wood shaft

grinding stones

iron axle

oil basin

Olive Fruit Pests

Olive fruit fly
(*Bactrocera oleae*)

One of the biggest olive tree pests is the olive fruit fly.
A female olive fruit fly lays eggs in olive flesh using an
ovipositor, a tube-shaped egg-laying **organ** at the rear
tip of her body. The egg hatches, or breaks open, two
or three days after it is laid, letting out a **maggot**. The
maggot feeds on the olive flesh for three weeks, leaving
tunnels in the olive flesh. When it has eaten enough,
the maggot becomes a **pupa** and stops eating for about
a week. Then the pupa becomes an adult fly and leaves
the olive. Although fruit fly tunnels cause no harm
to the olives at first, they often cause the olive to
begin rotting.

Common blackbird
(Turdus merula)

Birds that eat olives, like
the ones shown here, help
to spread olive seeds as well.
Birds fly to olive orchards
and eat the trees' fruit,
dropping the seeds under
other trees. Sometimes they
will carry the seeds several
miles away.

Other animals, like foxes,
also swallow whole olives and
the seeds come out in their
waste and enter the soil.

Song thrush
(Turdus philomelos)

Eurasian jay
*(Garrulus
glandarius)*

Athena Gave Us the Olive Tree

An ancient Greek tale says that Poseidon, god of the sea, gave people the first horse, but that Athena, the goddess of wisdom, or knowledge, gave people the first olive tree. For her gift, Athena became the goddess of Athens. To the ancient Western world, there was no tree more important than the olive.

Ancient Greeks used olive oil to light their lamps and oil their skin. Egyptian rulers who died were buried with art that featured images, or pictures, of olives. The doors to King Solomon's Temple were made from olive wood. Olive oil was traded all around the ancient world. Even today an olive branch is a common sign of peace.

Right: The back of an older U.S. quarter shows an eagle perched, or sitting, above an olive branch. The eagle stands for the nation's strength, while the olive branch stands for its wish for peace.

Olive trees have long been a favorite subject of artists. At left is a painting by Ambrogio Lorenzetti that uses the olive branch to stand for peace. Above it is a dove carrying an olive branch, a worldwide sign of peace, drawn by Pablo Picasso.

Opposite page: A painted vase shows an olive harvest in ancient Greece.

Glossary

chemical (KEH-mih-kul) One of the basic elements or building blocks of matter.

cultivating (KULL-ti-vayt-ing) Helping things grow; gardening.

droughts (DROWTS) Dry periods when little or no rain falls.

drupe (DROOP) A fleshy fruit that has a single hard pit.

embryo (EM-bree-oh) An animal or plant before it is born, when it is still in the egg, womb, or seed.

fertilizes (FUHR-tuhl-izez) Providing an ovule with the pollen material needed to produce a young plant.

grafted (GRAFT-ed) A branch from one tree joined to the trunk of another tree.

harvest (HAR-vist) To gather in a crop.

lye (LIE) A toxic substance used in making soap and curing some foods.

maggot (MA-guht) The larva, or first growth form, of a fly.

missionaries (MIH-shuh-ner-eez) People who travel away from their homes to teach other people about their beliefs in God.

organ (OR-gun) A group of cells or a body part that has a specific job to perform in the body.

ovary (OH-vuh-ree) The female part of a flower that grows up to become a fruit.

ovipositor (oh-vuh-PAWZ-ih-tuhr) An insect's egg-laying organ.

ovule (OV-yule) The part inside a plant ovary that grows up to become a seed.

perfect flowers (PUR-fect FLAU-erz) Flowers that have both male and female parts and can make pollen as well as seeds and fruits.

pollen (POLL-in) Tiny particles that carry a portion of the material needed to produce a plant seed.

pupa (PYOO-pah) The second stage in the growth of an insect.

stigmas (STIG-muhs) The portions of a female flower that catch pollen.

transplanted (tranz-PLANT-id) Uprooted and moved to new soil or a new location.

Index

Web Sites

Due to the changing nature of Internet links, PowerKids Press has developed an online list of Web sites related to the subject of this book. This site is updated regularly. Please use this link to access the list:

www.powerkidslinks.com/gin/oltr

About the Author

Andrew Hipp has been working as a naturalist in Madison, Wisconsin, since 1993. He is currently finishing his doctoral work in botany at the University of Wisconsin. Andrew and his wife, Rachel Davis, are collaborating on an illustrated field guide to common sedges of Wisconsin as they look forward to the birth of their first child.

Acknowledgments:
This book draws on research and writings by B. Avidan, L. Ferguson, M. Rosenblum, J. M. Taylor, C. Vitagliano, C. Voyiatzi, C. Xiloyannis, and their sources and collaborators. The author gratefully acknowledges Dr. Ferguson for reviewing a draft of this book.

Photo Credits